Anil was fed up, he was ill AGA
I can't go to Sammi's birthday party.

'It's not fair,' he moaned to his sister Anna. 'Why do I always get nasty colds?'

'You need to eat more fruit and vegetables,' said Anna.

'Sweets don't have any goodness in them, but fruits and vegetables contain lots of good things that our bodies need to keep us fit and healthy.'

Anil fell asleep dreaming about all the things that he could do if only he felt better...

HAPPY BIRTHD

He could see his friends but how could he get there?

'Follow the cucumber trail until you reach Strawberry Mountain,' said Mr Apple.

Can you help Anil to follow the right path?

DANGER
DANGER

Where next?
'Up here,'
said Mrs Peach.

'Follow the Kiwi Kids, then jump and catch the cauliflower cloud.'

Floating along on the cauliflower cloud, Anil looked down on the magical world of fruit and vegetables.

He could see:

the Banana Boys,

the Tomato Family,

the Grape Girls,

and the Sliding Sultanas

Suddenly the cloud was rising upwards over Pineapple Peak and it was beginning to rain raspberries.

'Quick, catch a raspberry,' cried Mr Pomegranate.

'A melon boat is waiting for you in Fruit Juice Lake.'

Anil sailed across the lake and can you guess who was waiting for him on Satsuma Sand?

Yes, his friends and they were singing a song.

Anil woke up with a start. It was all a dream, but he could still hear the song.